WHY KNOWING ISN'T ENOUGH

WHY KNOWING ISN'T ENOUGH

The No-Fluff Guide to Building a Business
That Finally Turns Actions Into Profits

GLENIS GASSMANN

www.glenisgassmann.com
www.yoursuccessshift.com

Copyright © 2025 Glenis Gassmann
All rights reserved.

No part of this publication may be reproduced, stored in a retrieval system, or transmitted in any form or by any means—electronic, mechanical, photocopying, recording, or otherwise—without the prior written permission of the publisher, except in the case of brief quotations embodied in reviews and articles.

This publication is intended for informational purposes only. The author and publisher make no guarantees of success or earnings. Business outcomes are dependent on individual decisions, actions, and external factors beyond the control of the author or publisher.

For permissions or inquiries, contact:
glenis@glenisgassmann.com
www.glenisgassmann.com

First Edition
ISBN: 978-0-9944807-2-9 (electronic)
ISBN: 978-0-9944807-3-6 (paperback)
Cover design by: 100 Covers
Edited by: Erik Seversen
Interior Formatting: Dindo Sanguenza
Australia

If you've picked up this book, chances are you already know quite a bit about what it takes to succeed in business.

You've read the books, attended the workshops, downloaded the templates. But something's still missing—and that "missing" isn't more information. It's traction.

This book isn't here to impress you. It's here to move you. To get you unstuck. To shift you from knowing what to do… to actually doing it—consistently, clearly, and with confidence.

Everything I share in these pages comes from working with real business owners—people just like you—who wanted more than just another strategy. They wanted results. And they were ready to do the work to get there.

So if you're feeling scattered, stuck, or stalled—know this: you're not alone, and you're not broken. You're simply ready for a different kind of guidance. One that meets you where you are and helps you move forward, one small, smart step at a time.

Let's shift your success—together.

DEDICATION

To my clients—

Thank you for the trust you've placed in me over the years. You've shared your wins, your struggles, your ideas, and your fears— and through that, you've given me the greatest gift of all: the insight and clarity to write this book.

Your courage to take action, your willingness to grow, and your commitment to doing the real work have deeply inspired me. This book exists because of you—your questions, your breakthroughs, your transformations.

You are the proof that knowing isn't enough. Doing is where the magic happens. And I'm honoured to have walked that journey with you.

With gratitude,

ABOUT THE AUTHOR
GLENIS GASSMANN

Glenis Gassmann is a business strategist, coach and mentor with over 35 years of hands-on experience in building, scaling and successfully exiting businesses. She hasn't just studied success—she's lived it, navigating the messy middle of entrepreneurship and discovering what actually drives results.

After founding a thriving accounting and coaching firm, Glenis worked with hundreds of business owners to identify untapped opportunities, implement high-impact changes and move from scattered effort to focused execution. Her secret? Helping clients cut through the noise, stop overthinking and finally act on what they already know works.

Today, Glenis is the founder of *Your Success Shift*, a results-focused coaching platform that empowers business owners to close the gap between intention and action. She is known for her straight-talking, practical approach to business growth—one that's grounded in clarity, consistency, and small, smart steps that compound.

This book reflects her life's work: guiding capable people to stop stalling and start building the business—and life—they truly want.

Learn more at: www.yoursuccessshift.com

INTRODUCTION

You don't need more ideas. You need to do something with the ones you already have.

The Missing Link Between Knowing What to Do—and Actually Doing It

How many times have you had a game-changing idea for your business—one that could increase your profits, expand your reach or finally free you from the daily grind—only to watch it fade into the background of your never-ending to-do list?

Be honest.

You've attended seminars, bought courses, read books and filled notebooks with strategies and tactics that could transform your business. You know what to do. Yet, for some reason, you're still stuck in the same business cycle—overloaded, second-guessing and struggling to implement what you've learned from the day-to-day overload.

You're not alone.

I've worked with hundreds of business owners who have been trapped in the same frustrating loop—armed with knowledge but lacking implementation skills. They aren't lazy. They aren't unmotivated. They're just stuck in the gap between knowing what to do and actually doing it.

But here's the truth:

Success isn't about how much you know—it's about what you consistently do. They say information is power, but its true power is only unlocked when you act consistently. The most successful business owners aren't necessarily the smartest, the most experienced or the most creative. They are the ones who take consistent, disciplined action—no matter what. They move forward, adjust and keep going while others hesitate, overthink and get buried in busywork.

The Leader Within You: Why We Struggle to Take Action

We live in a world where knowledge is abundant, yet action is scarce. Every day, business owners consume information, they attend seminars, read books and brainstorm ideas. Yet most of these insights never materialise into tangible results. Why?

Because taking action is not just about having the right strategies—it's about having the discipline, courage and integrity to consistently follow through, even when there's no immediate reward, no external validation, and no guarantee of success.

Most people don't struggle with knowing what to do; they struggle with actually doing it.

This book is for business owners, innovators, and change-makers who are tired of watching ideas stay stuck in their heads, on a piece of paper, in a file on their computer. It's for those who feel the pull to create something bigger, a shift in how things are done—but find themselves stopped by self-doubt, fear, procrastination or just dealing with the everyday grind.

Why Knowing Isn't Enough is not just a concept—it's a call to action. A challenge to step up, commit and become the kind of leader who doesn't just dream but does.

The Three-Part Framework: The Success Shift

This book is designed to help you break through everything that stops you; act and sustain it until it becomes second nature.

It is structured in three parts, guiding you step by step through the process.

Part 1 – The Psychology of Inaction: Understanding why we resist taking action, overcoming fear and shifting your mindset to break through hesitation.

Part 2 – Building Your Action System: Practical, proven steps to create momentum, stay disciplined and take consistent action without feeling overwhelmed.

Part 3 – Becoming an Action-Driven Leader: How to embed action as a habit in your daily life, led by example and inspire others to do the same.

By the time you finish this book, you won't just understand what it takes to succeed—you will be living it.

Why Do We Get Stuck?

If you've ever asked yourself:

- Why am I not following through on what I already know?
- Why do I get motivated, only to lose momentum?
- Why am I not getting the results I expected, even though I have the right strategy?

Then this book is for you.

It's not that you're lacking the right knowledge—you're lacking the right action system.

You're about to learn why our human nature often works against us when it comes to implementing change. Our brains are wired for comfort, safety and routine—even when those routines are keeping us stuck. But once you understand this, you can override those instincts and become the kind of business owner who makes things happen—no matter what.

The Success Shift: A Proven Action Framework

This book will guide you through a step-by-step process to bridge the gap between knowledge and action. It's not about just understanding action—it's about living it.

Inside, you'll discover:

- The psychology of inaction: Why we resist taking action and how to break through it
- How to build unshakeable discipline: Action becomes second nature
- The power of decision-making: How to move forward with confidence
- Why bold action trumps perfection: How to take action before you feel "ready"
- How to keep going when no one agrees: Developing the courage to move forward

Each chapter is designed to challenge you, shift your mindset and give you the tools to transform your business through action.

You'll also read real stories—mine and my clients'—of how we overcame hesitation, self-doubt and failure to build businesses that thrive through action, not just ideas.

Your Challenge: Commit to Doing

This book isn't just for reading—it's for implementing.

I challenge you to make this commitment right now:

- Decide that you will be the kind of business owner who takes action.
- Stop waiting for perfect conditions—start today, no matter how small.
- Refuse to let fear, overthinking or past failures hold you back.

By the time you finish this book, you won't just be thinking about success—you'll be living it.

Welcome to *Why Knowing Isn't Enough, Let's* make this shift together.

CONTENTS

Part 1: The Gap Between Knowing and Doing

Before we shift into action, we need to understand why we don't act. Human beings are wired for comfort, survival, and seeking the path of least resistance. Our brain's default mode is to protect us from discomfort, failure and risk—even when the discomfort of staying the same is far greater than the discomfort of change.

In this section, we'll break down the psychology of inaction, why we let ourselves off the hook, and how to override the mental patterns that keep us stuck in thinking instead of doing.

Chapter 1: Why We Get Stuck

- Understanding the brain's resistance to change
- The role of fear, doubt and self-sabotage in keeping us in place
- How past conditioning convinces us that our ideas won't work
- Breakthrough Mindset Shift: *You are not your thoughts. You are your actions.*

Chapter 2: The Power of Purpose

- Why discipline fails without a deep "WHY"
- Aligning your personal mission with your business vision
- The emotional force that pulls you into action
- Breakthrough Mindset Shift: *Clarity of purpose beats willpower every time.*

Part 2: The Framework for the Success Shift

Once you understand why inaction happens, it's time to break the cycle and shift into consistent execution. This framework is designed to create an unshakeable foundation for turning ideas into reality.

Chapter 3: Integrity – The Foundation of Action

- How keeping small promises to yourself builds trust
- The hidden cost of broken commitments
- Aligning your actions with your values to create unstoppable momentum
- Action Step: *Identify and eliminate habits of self-betrayal*

Chapter 4: Decision and Commitment – The Moment Everything Changes

- Success is not about having more options—it's about choosing and committing
- Why the fear of making the wrong choice is keeping you paralysed
- The moment you decide to burn the boats and go all in

- Action Step: *Create a non-negotiable decision for your next step*

Chapter 5: Bold Execution – Leading Without Agreement

- Why waiting for approval or consensus will kill your momentum
- The courage to take action when others don't see the vision yet
- How to push forward even when there is no evidence it will work
- Action Step: *Make one bold move today, without waiting for permission*

Chapter 6: Discipline – The Art of Taking Action Daily

- Why motivation is a myth and consistency wins
- Building unshakeable daily habits that make action second nature
- The role of environment, routines, and accountability
- Action Step: *Implement the "No Matter What" Daily Action Plan*

Chapter 7: Courage – Continuing in the Face of No Agreement

- What to do when others doubt you, dismiss you or say it won't work
- How to separate external rejection from your internal commitment

- Developing resilience to keep moving forward, even when progress feels invisible
- Action Step: *Identify where you're seeking approval instead of taking action*

Part 3: The Leadership Challenge – Becoming the Change-Maker

Success isn't about a one-time effort; it's about showing up, taking action and leading consistently until it becomes second nature—a habit so deeply ingrained that action becomes automatic, not something you have to force.

Chapter 8: Saying No to Distractions, Saying Yes to Your Mission

- The power of ruthless focus
- Why most people quit right before the breakthrough
- How to say NO to what doesn't serve your mission
- Action Step: *Identify three things to eliminate from your life immediately*

Chapter 9: Failure as Fuel – The Secret to Long-Term Success

- Why failure is a requirement, not a setback
- How successful leaders reframe failure into learning
- The ritual of reviewing, refining and relaunching
- Action Step: *Create a fail-forward log to track lessons, not losses*

Chapter 10: Lighting the Path for Others

- True leadership is not about doing it alone
- How to bring others into your vision
- The responsibility of creating change beyond yourself
- Action Step: *Identify who you can inspire to take action today*

Final Call to Action: The Success Shift Challenge

At the end of this book, you won't just walk away with ideas—you'll walk away with a challenge:

- Choose one thing you've been sitting on for too long.
- Decide to take action within the next 24 hours.
- Make a public commitment (to yourself, your network, or your team).
- Keep going—even when no one agrees, even when it's hard, even when you want to quit.

Because the world doesn't change with ideas—it changes with ACTION

CHAPTER 1

WHY WE GET STUCK

"The chains of habit are too light to be felt until they are too heavy to be broken."

—Warren Buffett

The Business Owner Who Meant Well — But Never Started

Meet David. He was a business owner with a big heart, tireless hustle and an even bigger vision. On paper, everything looked good. His consulting firm was respected and thriving. Clients loved him. His calendar stayed full. He had loyal relationships, strong referrals, and a business model that others envied.

But beneath the surface, something wasn't quite right.

David wasn't making progress. His days bled into each other, filled with back-to-back calls, inbox firefights and client needs that never seemed to end. He had a brilliant idea for a new premium service—one that could double his revenue and reduce his hours. He'd mapped out the plan. Blocked time in the calendar. Even visualised the impact it could have.

And yet… nothing.

Each time he sat down to begin, something urgent would hijack his attention—a last-minute client request, a staffing issue, an unexpected tech hiccup. "I'll do it next week," he'd promise himself.

But next week never came.

The truth? David wasn't unmotivated. He wasn't lazy. He was one of the most dedicated entrepreneurs I'd ever met. But like so many others, he had become a master of *maintenance*—not momentum. He kept everything running smoothly, but never had time to build what was next.

David was stuck in what I call the Busy Work Cycle—where constant activity disguises the absence of real progress. Urgency always wins. Importance always waits.

And if you've ever felt like David… you're not alone.

The Vision Board Trap—Samantha's Story

Samantha was the opposite of stuck—or so it seemed. She was creative, radiant and full of passion. Each year, she'd create a breathtaking vision board, brimming with magazine clippings, quotes, handwritten goals and strategic ideas. Her planner was colour-coded with intention. Her journal was filled with insights and mantras. Her whiteboard? A museum of genius waiting to be realised.

But something strange kept happening.

Year after year, despite the vision, her business stayed in the same place. She always *almost launched* something new. Always *almost rebranded*. Always *almost scaled* her services.

The problem wasn't ambition—Samantha had plenty.

The problem was *execution*. Samantha was spending 95% of her energy dreaming, organising and planning—and only 5% actually doing. Her days felt productive, but her output told a different story. She was always preparing, but rarely publishing. Always mapping, but rarely moving.

Then one afternoon, sitting in front of another beautifully outlined but untouched project plan, she asked herself a powerful question: "What if I just did one thing today—no matter how small or imperfect?"

So, she did. She sent one email. She put up a rough version of her sales page. She posted one message to her community. The sky didn't fall. The plan wasn't perfect. But she made progress—real, measurable, momentum-building progress.

That single imperfect action became the crack in the dam. The flood of results followed—first sales, new clients, a simplified offer that finally took off. Samantha learned what so many of us need to hear: Action beats organisation. Execution beats intention.

Reflection Prompt: Samantha's Story

Samantha's turning point came not from a bigger plan, but a smaller step. Her decision to act—even without perfection—created momentum no vision board ever could.

Take a moment to reflect:

- Are you spending more time *planning* success than actually *pursuing* it?
- What's one small, messy, imperfect action you could take this week that would move you closer to your goal?

Write it down.

Then take it.

The Science of Why We Stay Stuck

There's a biological reason most of us get trapped in maintenance mode.

Your brain is wired for survival, not success. When you face something new or unfamiliar—like launching a new service, raising your prices, or finally building that automated funnel—your brain sees *risk*, not opportunity. Even when the logical part of your mind wants to move forward, your subconscious leans into protection.

So, instead of taking bold action, your brain urges you to:

- Focus on short-term tasks that feel "productive".
- Avoid high-effort, high-reward projects.
- Delay big decisions because uncertainty feels unsafe.

This is why so many business owners live in *reaction mode*. They work in their business… but rarely on it.

Here's the hard truth: If you don't make time for growth, it won't happen. The right time will never appear. You have to create it.

Breaking Free: The First Mindset Shift

If there's one message I want you to remember from this book, it's this: You must become the kind of business owner who takes action *before* you feel ready.

That means making some key mindset shifts:

- Stop mistaking *busywork* for real progress.
- Accept that *discomfort* is part of the growth process.
- Schedule your most important actions *first*—and stick to them, even when easier tasks call your name.

If it's important, it gets scheduled. If it's scheduled, it gets done. Make that your mantra—and you'll immediately set yourself apart from 95% of business owners stuck in planning mode.

Deep Dive: The Busy Work Trap

Busy work is a seductive trap. It feels productive. It gives you little wins. It fills your day. But most of the time, it keeps you comfortable—not successful.

Signs you're stuck in busy work:

- You finish each day exhausted but unsure what you actually accomplished.
- You answer every email, attend every meeting and check every notification—but never make progress on big goals.
- You procrastinate the important work by doing the easy work first… and never get around to what really matters.

Morning Audit Prompt: Before you begin your workday, ask yourself, "Is this task moving me closer to my biggest goal, or just keeping me busy?"

Choosing discomfort—even once a day—compounds faster than you think.

Reflection Prompt: Where Am I Stuck?

Let's get honest:

- Where am I spending more time—planning or doing?
- What's one important action I keep avoiding?
- When do I tend to reach for busywork instead of bold moves?
- What would it feel like to make *progress* over chasing perfection?
- What's possible for me if I shifted my focus from preparation to execution?

Don't overthink it. Jot down a few thoughts. Awareness is the first step to momentum.

Your First Success Shift Challenge: Get Unstuck Now

Let's move from reflection to action—right now.

The 6-Minute Rule

Choose one small business-growth task you've been putting off. It might be:

- Starting the proposal.
- Reaching out to a potential client.
- Mapping a new offer.

Set a timer for six minutes.

Start immediately—no overthinking, no stalling.

You don't need to finish. The goal is simply to *start*. Why? Because once you begin, your brain shifts from fear to focus.

Momentum is built in minutes—not hours.

Success Requires Support

If six minutes of focused action can shift your energy… imagine what a consistent system of support, accountability and execution could do. The biggest reason business owners stay stuck? They try to do it all alone. But successful leaders don't walk solo. They surround themselves with people who push them forward, challenge their blind spots and keep them focused when life gets noisy.

In the chapters ahead, we'll explore how to build systems that support execution—so you can consistently follow through on your best ideas.

But before we go there, you have one job:

Complete your 6-minute challenge.

Today. Not later. Not tomorrow. Because real success doesn't come from what you know. It comes from what you do.

If you are looking for a simple and powerful mental model to help you turn this chapter into real progress, try the "Clarity Tonic" below. All the success shift recipes are located at www. http://www.yoursuccessshift.com/recipes to help you turn insight into momentum.

Clarity Tonic

Purpose: Sets the tone for intentional action

Ingredients:

- 1 cup of radical honesty
- 2 teaspoons of self-awareness
- A generous squeeze of fresh perspective
- Optional: a sprig of excitement for the journey ahead

Method:

- Stir together honesty and awareness to identify where you're stuck.
- Add perspective to reframe your current stage.
- Sip slowly—this is just the beginning.

Serving Suggestion:

- Best enjoyed with quiet reflection and a willingness to begin.

CHAPTER 2

THE POWER OF PURPOSE — "YOUR WHY" IS THE KEY TO TAKING ACTION

"Start with why. People don't buy what you do; they buy why you do it."

—Simon Sinek

The Moment Everything Changed for Me

I didn't start my business because I wanted to "be my own boss". I didn't do it for more time or less stress. In fact, in those early years, I worked harder and longer than I ever did in a 9-to-5 job.

The real reason I started?

I wanted flexibility. Not just for me—for my family.

I remember it vividly. My daughter had chickenpox, and I had no family nearby to help. My boss, instead of showing understanding, expected me to come into work anyway. I felt trapped—torn between being a mother and an employee, forced to choose between my child's needs and a job that paid the bills.

That moment broke something open in me. I knew I never wanted to be in that position again. I resigned two months later and started my own business—not to chase a title, but to build a life on my own terms.

At first, I thought *that* was my why. But over time, I realised my deeper purpose was much bigger than just flexibility or freedom. As I grew, I came across Simon Sinek's *Start with Why*, and it stirred something powerful inside me. I began asking deeper questions: Why do business owners really go into business? And why do so many feel like they're still stuck—even after making the leap?

The answer? Most entrepreneurs begin with a desire for freedom, but quickly find themselves shackled by the very thing they built. They work more hours than ever. They serve clients that control their time. They stay in survival mode, rather than creating the vision they once imagined.

That's when I discovered my true purpose:

To lead and empower others to step into their own potential and take full responsibility for creating a business—and life—aligned with who they truly are.

Because without a strong, soul-driven *why*… execution will always be a struggle.

Marcus' Wake-Up Call—From Hustle to Heart

Marcus looked like the poster child of entrepreneurial success. He owned one of the top fitness studios in town. His face was featured on local TV, he had brand deals with major wellness companies, and his lifestyle seemed enviable.

But behind the polished surface, Marcus was barely holding it together. Fuelled by coffee, stress and endless to-do lists, he ran at full speed—

chasing growth, expansion, more visibility, more wins. He worked seven days a week, convincing himself it was "all for the family". But slowly, the people he said he was doing it for began to drift away.

Family birthdays blurred into business meetings. Quality time became occasional text check-ins. He missed more moments than he remembered.

Then came the breaking point. On a sunny Saturday afternoon, Marcus had a chance to close a lucrative corporate wellness deal—a deal he told himself would "take everything to the next level". But that same afternoon, his son played in his very first soccer match. He scored his first goal.

Marcus wasn't there. That night, he came home to find a crumpled team photo on the kitchen counter. His son had written his name in shaky handwriting along the bottom. Marcus sat in the dark, holding that photo in silence. His heart cracked open. He realised that while he had been building an empire, he had been neglecting the very people that made it all worth it. The business was thriving—but his joy, his relationships and his sense of presence were collapsing.

That night became his wake-up call. Marcus made a radical shift. He simplified his business model. He hired support. He stopped chasing "more" and started protecting what mattered most. No more work on weekends. No more constant availability. He drew firm, life-affirming boundaries around his time and energy.

And something unexpected happened. Not only did Marcus find peace—his business doubled in revenue. His energy changed. His clarity attracted aligned opportunities and loyal clients. When he led with heart, success followed.

Marcus learned what many business owners realise only too late: A business that costs you your life isn't success—it's slow collapse.

Reflection Prompt: Marcus' Wake-Up Call

Marcus discovered that *presence* matters more than *performance*. His wake-up call was clear: building a business at the expense of what you love is not success—it's misalignment.

Take a moment to reflect:

- Is the life you're building today making space for the moments you'll want to remember tomorrow?
- What's one boundary you could set—or reset—that would protect what truly matters to you?

Andrew's Leap—Trading Bureaucracy for Real Purpose

Andrew did everything "right". After 20 years in corporate, he had earned the title, the office, the salary, the status. His résumé was polished. His track record, impressive.

But inside? He was suffocating.

His days were consumed by meetings, politics and approvals. Progress moved at a snail's pace. Ideas were routinely diluted or dismissed. Service to customers had become secondary to preserving internal processes. Most days, Andrew felt like he was managing *process*, not creating *impact*.

The environment drained him. Collaboration felt like competition. Recognition was hollow. The spark that had once lit him up was long gone.

And then came the quiet, powerful question: *Is this really how I want to spend the rest of my life?*

He began imagining a different future—one where his work meant something again. Where his expertise helped real businesses, real leaders, and real people. A future where progress didn't need a committee.

He dreamed of starting a consulting business. Something simple. Purposeful. Free of politics and full of impact.

But fear kept whispering:

- *What if I'm too old to start again?*
- *What if I fail without corporate safety?*

Then, one night, staring at yet another quarterly report that nobody cared about, the truth dropped into his heart: *If I could end each day knowing I made a real difference—that would be enough.*

That clarity cut through the fear. He didn't need a perfect plan. He needed alignment.

Andrew leapt. He quit, started small, and focused on impact over image. The path wasn't smooth—but it was *his*. And slowly, purpose replaced politics. Clients came. Fulfilment returned.

And for the first time in decades, Andrew felt alive in his work.

Reflection Prompt: Andrew's Leap

Andrew's story reminds us that titles and salaries can't replace meaning. At the end of the day, the question isn't: *What do I do?* It's: *Why does it matter?*

Reflect on this:

- If your job title disappeared, would your current work still feel meaningful?
- If not, what's one small step you could take this week to move towards more aligned, purpose-driven work?

Why We Fail to Follow Through

Think about the last big goal you set. Maybe it was launching a new offer. Scaling your team. Creating a better work-life balance. You started strong. You felt excited. You made a plan. But then? Life happened. Emails piled up. Urgent tasks took over. And motivation faded.

Sounds familiar?

Here's the truth most people avoid: **If your WHY isn't strong enough, your follow-through won't last.**

Motivation is fleeting. But purpose is fuel.

Deep Dive: Surface Whys vs. Soulful Whys

Surface Whys:

- Make more money
- Get validation
- Look successful
- Prove someone wrong

Soulful Whys:

- Freedom
- Fulfilment
- Legacy
- Self-expression
- Contribution

How do you know the difference?

Surface Whys often feel hollow. You hit the goal and still feel unsatisfied. Soulful Whys energise you. They pull you forward when things get hard. If your WHY gives you goosebumps or tears… you've found it.

Reflection Prompt: Digging into Your Own Why

Ask yourself honestly:

- Why did I start (or grow) this business in the first place?
- How has my WHY evolved over time?
- Where am I still operating from fear or ego, instead of heart and purpose?
- What would change if I made decisions from my deepest WHY—not just survival or success?
- What's one step I can take this week to honour my *real* reason for doing this?

Your Success Shift Challenge: The 7 Layers of Why

To move from *knowing* to *doing*, you need a WHY that anchors you.

Here's your challenge: **The 7 Layers of Why Exercise**

Ask yourself: *Why do I want to grow my business?*

Ask: *Why is that important to me?*

Then ask again: *Why does that matter?*

Repeat this process seven times.

By the 7th answer, you'll feel it. It will land deeper. That's your real WHY.

Pro Tip: Your real WHY is rarely about money. It's about freedom, meaning, identity, or love.

Write it down. Revisit it daily. Let it guide your decisions. Because when your WHY is soul-deep, action becomes non-negotiable.

And execution? It becomes who you are—not just something you try to do.

If you are looking for a simple and powerful mental model to help you turn this chapter into real progress, try the "Busywork Stir-Fry" below. All the success shift recipes are located at http://www.yoursuccessshift.com/recipes to help you turn insight into momentum.

Busywork Stir-Fry

Purpose: Highlights the chaos of doing without moving

Ingredients:

- 1 overflowing plate of to-dos
- A dash of distraction
- 2 tablespoons of avoidance seasoning
- Replace with 1 core task that matters

Method:

- Toss out distractions and simmer down the task list.
- Keep only what moves you forward.
- Serve one key project hot and fresh.

Serving Suggestion:

- Use the 6-minute rule as your kitchen timer.

CHAPTER 3

BUILDING INTEGRITY—WHY DOING WHAT YOU SAY MATTERS MORE THAN YOU THINK

"You are what you do, not what you say you'll do."

—Carl Jung

Integrity: The Hidden Engine of Success

In business, we often imagine success as the result of grand strategies, brilliant marketing or groundbreaking ideas. But if you scratch the surface of every truly successful entrepreneur, leader or visionary, you'll find something far more fundamental: They consistently do what they say they will do.

Integrity isn't just about being honest with others—it's about being honest with yourself. It's the quiet alignment between your words, your intentions, and your actions. When you consistently follow through on your commitments—even the small, "no one will know if I don't" kind— you build unstoppable momentum. You create evidence that you are trustworthy. You build the foundation for boldness, creativity and growth.

When you don't? You quietly erode your own self-trust—the very fuel you need in order to take risks, face challenges and build something meaningful.

Self-trust is the foundation of confidence, action, and resilience. Without it, even the best strategies in the world will feel too heavy to execute.

Emma's Confidence Comeback

Emma was a gifted graphic designer. Her work was stunning—thoughtful, expressive and bold. Clients who worked with her sang her praises, and her portfolio overflowed with creative brilliance. But behind the screen, Emma was caught in a quiet battle with herself—one that had nothing to do with skill and everything to do with self-doubt.

She hesitated when it came time to submit proposals, questioning if they were "good enough". She would delay sending completed designs, endlessly tweaking them, chasing a version of perfection that always seemed one edit away. She regularly turned down larger opportunities, quietly telling herself, "I'm not ready yet." On the surface, it seemed like a confidence problem. But beneath that hesitation was something deeper.

With the support of a trusted mentor, Emma began to unpack the real story—and what she uncovered surprised her. Her confidence wasn't lacking because of her abilities; it was crumbling because of a pattern she hadn't even noticed. She had, over time, developed a habit of breaking promises to herself.

They were small at first. She told herself she'd update her portfolio over the weekend—but didn't. She planned to pitch to three new clients by the end of the month—then let fear or busyness get in the way. She set intentions at the start of each month that quietly dissolved by week two. These weren't just missed tasks—they were unspoken messages to herself: *You don't follow through. You can't be trusted.*

And that internal narrative, though subtle, had weight. Every unkept promise chipped away at her self-belief. Every postponed goal reinforced the idea that she wasn't capable of delivering—not just to others, but to herself.

When Emma saw this clearly, she made a powerful but deceptively simple decision: she would only commit to what she knew she would follow through on—no matter how small. She stopped setting grand targets she couldn't meet and started honouring micro-promises with radical consistency.

If she committed to sending one email per day, she sent it—even if it felt too small to matter. If she told herself she would update one page of her portfolio, she updated it—no delays, no excuses. If she agreed to reach out to just one new potential client each week, she did it—rain, hail, or shine.

And then something shifted. Within six months, her confidence returned—and this time, it wasn't tied to results or validation. It came from the inside. Her client base doubled. She no longer second-guessed herself at every turn. She moved faster, trusted her instincts and began saying *yes* to opportunities she had once backed away from. But the biggest transformation wasn't professional—it was personal. She fell back in love with her work. And with herself.

Emma didn't reinvent who she was. She simply changed how she related to herself. She became a woman who kept her word—especially to herself. And that changed everything. Because confidence isn't built by being perfect. It's built by proving to yourself, over and over, that you'll show up.

Reflection Prompt: Emma's Confidence Comeback

Emma's story reminds us that confidence isn't something we're born with or something we wait to earn—it's something we build by keeping our word to ourselves, one small action at a time.

Take a moment to reflect:

- Are you making promises to yourself that you consistently break?
- What is *one small commitment* you can make this week—and fully honour—to begin rebuilding trust in yourself?

My Personal Wake-Up Call Around Integrity

Before I stepped into the world of business coaching, I led a successful accounting firm. On paper, we had everything dialled in: the latest systems, state-of-the-art technology, a loyal client base, and a solid vision for where we were heading. From the outside, we looked like a well-oiled machine.

But beneath the surface, I began noticing subtle cracks. Productivity was lagging. Team morale felt inconsistent. Accountability, ownership, and a sense of responsibility weren't showing up the way I knew they needed to. At first, it was easy to point fingers. I saw deadlines being missed, blame being passed around like a hot potato, and stories being spun about why tasks hadn't been completed—with little regard for how those delays affected the broader team or our clients.

I could have stayed in blame. But something in me—something deeper—knew better.

Leadership starts at the top. So, I did what most leaders avoid when things go sideways: I turned the mirror inwards. And what I saw was humbling.

I realised I wasn't always on time for meetings. I sometimes allowed my diary to overrun, leaving clients or team members waiting. I wasn't checking in consistently on open client jobs, assuming instead that everyone shared my sense of urgency and drive. I had unknowingly created space for excuses by modelling a standard that was just slightly out of alignment.

The truth hit me hard: I wasn't fully walking the talk. And that disconnect was rippling through the business. That moment—bitter as it was—became a powerful turning point. I made a conscious decision: if I wanted my team to show up with ownership, clarity and integrity, I had to fully embody those qualities first.

So I made some changes. I added breathing space between appointments to ensure I wasn't rushing—or running late. I began holding short, daily stand-ups with the team to keep communication sharp and remove roadblocks early. I even started walking faster through the office—not out of stress, but as a visual signal of momentum, energy and urgency.

And slowly, something shifted. The team began mirroring the change. Meetings started on time. Project updates came without prompting. Instead of blame, there were real conversations. Instead of silence or delay, there was action. We hadn't just improved performance—we had transformed the culture.

We chose *Integrity* as a company value—not as a nice-sounding word on the wall, but as a lived standard. And when someone couldn't keep their word, we didn't shame them—we created a structure. A simple, human process for re-communicating early, resetting expectations, and reducing impact. That one change alone elevated how we related to each other and to our work.

This experience taught me something I've never forgotten: integrity isn't about perfection. It's about responsibility. It's about owning your word—and your impact—in a way that builds trust, inspires excellence, and brings out the best in those around you.

It changed our business. It changed our team. And it changed me.

Reflection Prompt

Integrity isn't about being flawless—it's about taking responsibility for how your actions (and inactions) impact others. True leadership begins when you consistently model the standards you expect from those around you.

Take a moment to reflect:

- Where in your work or life are you expecting others to show up fully—without holding yourself to the same standard?
- What's one small shift you can make this week to better model the culture or values you want to see in your team or relationships?

The Invisible Cost of Broken Micro-Promises

Every time you break a promise to yourself, even a tiny one, it leaves a mark. It quietly teaches your mind a dangerous lesson: "Your words don't mean much." The impact isn't immediate. But over time, it accumulates into a heavy emotional burden:

You start to think:

- "I never stick to anything."
- "I'm not disciplined."
- "I can't trust myself."

And when you believe those thoughts? You procrastinate. You hesitate. You avoid opportunities. You shrink to fit the story you've told yourself.

But there's another way.

When you *keep* your promises—even micro-promises—you build a different identity entirely.

You start to think:

- "I do what I say."
- "I can rely on myself."
- "I'm building something, even if it's brick by brick."

Keeping your word isn't just about productivity. It's about identity. It's about becoming the kind of person who can create extraordinary results because they trust themselves to act when it matters most. Confidence isn't built by achieving huge goals overnight. Confidence is built by honouring small commitments consistently. And confidence leads to action. Action leads to results. Results lead to transformation.

Reflection: Where Am I Out of Integrity?

Take a moment to reflect honestly.

- Where in my life or business have I been breaking small promises to myself or others?
- What excuses have I been telling myself to justify it?
- How does it feel inside when I keep a commitment, even a tiny one?
- What area of my life would transform if I rebuilt trust with myself?
- What is one micro-promise I can make—and keep—today?

Write down your thoughts. Awareness is the first step towards lasting change.

Your Success Shift Challenge: Micro-Promise Mastery

If you want to move from *knowing* to *doing*, you must first rebuild trust with the most important person in your business journey: yourself.

Here's how…

Challenge: Choose Your Micro-Promise

Pick one tiny action you will commit to for the next 7 days. It should be small enough that you'd feel silly *not* doing it—but meaningful enough that it strengthens your self-trust muscle.

Examples:

- Write for 6 minutes every morning.
- Send one value-adding message per day.
- Spend 6 minutes planning tomorrow's top priority before you log off.
- Drink one extra glass of water each day.
- Spend 5 minutes each evening tidying your workspace.

Rule: Once You Choose It, You Must Honour It

No matter how you feel. No matter how busy you are. No matter what excuses pop up. This is how you show yourself that your word *means something*. Because when your words and actions are in sync, you become unstoppable.

Final Thought: The Snowball of Self-Trust

Imagine your promises as tiny snowflakes. Alone, they seem insignificant. But when you honour them, they start to stick together. Layer by layer, they form a snowball of self-trust that grows bigger, faster and more powerful with every small action. Soon, momentum is on your side. Confidence becomes your natural state. And achieving your goals becomes not a question of *if*, but *when*. When you trust yourself, momentum becomes inevitable.

If you are looking for a simple and powerful mental model to help you turn this chapter into real progress, try the "Action Cookies" below. All the success shift recipes are located at http://www.yoursuccessshift.com/recipes to help you turn insight into momentum.

Action Cookies

Purpose: Encourages imperfect action

Ingredients:

- 1 imperfect idea
- 1 spoon of courage
- A handful of messy progress
- Optional icing: public commitment

Method:

- Mix idea and courage—don't overthink.
- Drop into bite-sized steps.
- Bake for 6 minutes of action.

Serving Suggestion:

- Best when shared with a friend for accountability.

CHAPTER 4

DECISION AND COMMITMENT – THE POWER OF MOVING FORWARD

"The only limit to our realisation of tomorrow is our doubts of today".

—Franklin D. Roosevelt

The Business Owner Who Got Stuck in "One More Thing" Syndrome

Lisa was a brilliant entrepreneur with a bold vision. Her idea had the potential to shift the landscape of her industry—fresh, innovative, and deeply needed. She had the kind of clarity many business owners would envy. She knew what she wanted to build, and she was genuinely excited to bring it to life.

Lisa wasn't reckless or impulsive. In fact, she was the opposite. She did her homework diligently. She read the books, studied the market, listened to podcasts, interviewed experts, and crafted a detailed, thoughtful business plan. Everything seemed to be lining up for a strong launch. But something kept getting in the way.

Just when it was time to take action, Lisa would pause. "I just need to read one more book on marketing," she'd say. Or, "I should probably take another course before I start promoting." Sometimes it was, "Let me analyse the market a little longer to make sure it's the right time." And so it went—day after day, week after week, always circling back to *just one more thing*.

She was caught in a loop. Not because she lacked knowledge, but because she doubted her ability to move forward without perfect certainty. The deeper truth? Lisa wasn't preparing anymore—she was procrastinating in disguise.

Time passed. Months blurred into a full year. And while she continued perfecting her plan, she watched others bring similar ideas to market—ideas that looked strikingly like her own. They were gaining traction, building communities and earning revenue, while Lisa remained on the sidelines.

Eventually, she confided in me. "I don't understand," she said, frustration in her voice. "I'm smart. I work hard. I've done all the right things. But I just can't seem to pull the trigger."

I asked her a simple, but confronting question: "How much more information do you really need before you choose to act?"

She paused. And in that silence, the truth landed. Lisa realised that her ongoing research wasn't about getting ready anymore—it had become a shield. A way to avoid the discomfort of committing. A way to delay facing the risk that comes with showing up, being seen, and possibly failing.

That moment of clarity shifted everything. Lisa made a new decision: she would launch her offer—even if it wasn't perfect, even if she still felt uncertain. She chose movement over mastery. Action over avoidance. Courage over control. And something beautiful happened.

Her launch wasn't flawless, but it was real. Within six months, she had a growing client base, glowing testimonials and steady income. While others were still "getting ready", Lisa was serving her market, learning in real time, and building momentum. Her success didn't come from knowing more. It came from choosing to act on what she already knew—and backing herself in the process.

Reflection Prompt: Lisa's Story—One More Thing Syndrome

Lisa's story reminds us that preparation can quietly become procrastination—and that perfection is often just fear in disguise. At some point, choosing to act is the most powerful decision you can make.

Take a moment to reflect:

- Are you using "just one more thing" as a reason to delay taking action?
- What's one step you could take this week—even if it's imperfect—that would move you closer to launching or committing to your next big idea?

The Architect Who Waited Too Long

Thomas was a gifted architect—meticulous, creative, and deeply passionate about his craft. He had an eye for detail that few could rival and a vision for design that pushed the boundaries of form and function. His dream was clear: to launch his own boutique architecture firm. Not just another studio, but a place where design met meaning—a business that reflected his values, style and purpose.

He wasn't lacking in experience or skill. In fact, he had more knowledge and technical expertise than most of his peers. Years of training, award-winning projects, glowing client reviews—Thomas had built a solid foundation. Everyone around him assumed it was only a matter of time before he took the leap. But time kept passing.

Whenever the topic of launching came up, Thomas always had a reason to delay—reasonable, logical, intelligent reasons. He wanted to take one more certification, just to be "extra credible". He wanted to revise his business plan one last time. He wanted to gather a few more case studies to showcase the full breadth of his work. There was always something to polish, another gap to close.

He was always "almost ready…", but never moving. Weeks turned into months. Months turned into a couple of years. His dream sat quietly in a folder on his desktop, waiting for the right moment. And underneath all the preparation was a quiet fear—fear of putting himself out there without guarantees, fear of judgment, fear of not being enough when it finally mattered.

Then, during a mentoring session, someone asked him a simple but piercing question: "If you had to start today with everything you already know—what's the smallest project you could offer safely?" It stopped him in his tracks. For a moment, Thomas considered all the reasons why he shouldn't start. Then he realised that he already had what he needed to begin. Maybe not to build the full vision just yet—but enough to get moving.

So he did something he hadn't allowed himself to do before. He reached out to a local community project—a small-scale development that needed architectural input on a limited budget. It wasn't high-profile. It didn't demand perfection. But it was real. That one small commitment changed everything.

Thomas received immediate feedback—practical, grounded and invaluable. He navigated real challenges and adapted in real time. His confidence grew, not because he'd mastered more theory, but because he was finally applying what he knew. His ideas were no longer trapped in planning mode—they were out in the world, shaping spaces and making a difference.

Today, Thomas leads a thriving boutique architecture firm. He's worked on projects that inspire him, built a strong reputation, and carved out a space that is uniquely his. But his success didn't come from having it all figured out. It came the moment he stopped waiting for perfection—and started working with enough.

Reflection Prompt: Thomas's Story

Thomas's journey reminds us that waiting for perfection can become an obstacle to progress. His breakthrough came when he embraced the idea of starting small—with what he already had—rather than waiting for everything to be flawless.

Take a moment to reflect:

- In your own projects or aspirations, how often do you delay action in pursuit of perfection?
- What's one small, manageable step you could take today that would move you forward—even if it isn't perfect?

From Information Gathering to Informed Commitment

Gathering information is smart. It's responsible to educate yourself, weigh your options and approach your goals with care. But there's a line between preparation and paralysis—and many business owners cross it without even realising. There comes a point when more information doesn't help. It hurts.

Once you've gathered enough to move forward with reasonable safety—financially, legally, emotionally—not acting becomes the bigger risk. Too many entrepreneurs treat research like a fortress. They believe that if they gather enough facts, they'll make the leap without any fear. But business doesn't work that way.

Informed commitment is about recognising when you've reached enough. It's the moment you realise:

- You are no longer ignorant.
- You've done the foundational work.
- Your next level of growth can only be accessed through movement.

Choosing to act doesn't mean ignoring facts—it means trusting that you're ready enough to learn the rest through experience. Because the truth is: Clarity, refinement and mastery only show up after you move. Never before.

Why Business Owners Struggle with Commitment

Business owners love options. And they really love staying open to all of them: "I'll wait and see."; "I'll think about it."; "I'll get more advice first." It feels safer to delay. It feels riskier to commit, but here's the thing most people don't admit: Not making a decision is a decision.

And usually, it's a decision to stay stuck. Indecision isn't neutral. It drains your energy. It creates anxiety. It quietly chips away at your self-trust. The longer you hesitate, the louder the fear grows—and the harder it becomes to break free.

The Cost of Indecision

Every day you avoid making a decision, you lose more than time. You lose: *Confidence*: Every moment of hesitation tells your subconscious you can't trust yourself to follow through.

Opportunities: While you're "thinking it over", someone else is already out there doing it. *Momentum*: And momentum is everything. Without movement, your energy stagnates. Your ideas stall. Your progress fades.

Imagine two business owners with the same great idea: One chooses, launches, learns, and evolves. The other waits, plans, tweaks, and overthinks.

Six months later, one has customers, revenue, and feedback. The other has a perfect plan—and nothing else.

Which one would you rather be?

The Power of Committed Choices

Successful business owners don't get stuck in endless loops of preparation. They don't need 100% certainty before moving. What they do have is a deep trust in their ability to figure things out along the way. They commit with clarity. They act from alignment—not fear. They move with confidence—even when uncertainty remains. Because commitment isn't about having every answer in advance. It's about choosing a direction, backing yourself fully and adjusting as you go. And once you commit, something powerful happens:

- Doors open.
- People show up.
- Resources become available.

Movement creates momentum. Momentum creates opportunity.

The Commitment Shift: How to Choose and Move Forward Fast

If you want to shift from stuck to successful, here's a simple framework:

Step 1: Give Yourself a Deadline

Without a deadline, decisions stretch endlessly. Use timeframes like:

- Small choices → Commit within 5 minutes
- Medium choices → Commit within 24 hours
- Big, life-altering choices → Decide within a week

Still feeling torn? Flip a coin—not to make the decision, but to see how you feel about the outcome. Your gut knows what you want.

Step 2: Commit 100%

Once you choose, treat it like it's the best decision you could possibly make. Go all in. Back yourself. Adjust as needed—but stop second-guessing.

Step 3: Take Immediate Action

Don't wait. Lock in your decision by doing something now.

Send the email. Make the call. Post the offer.

Action fuels commitment—and builds self-trust faster than anything else.

Your Success Shift Challenge: The 24-Hour Committed Choice Rule

This is your invitation to move.

The 24-Hour Challenge

Choose something you've been delaying.

- Set a 24-hour deadline to decide.
- Make the best decision you can with what you already know.
- Take one immediate action to reinforce it.
- Tell someone for accountability.

Examples:

Been thinking about launching a program? Announce it.

Hesitating on a partnership? Say yes or no.

Sitting on a marketing idea? Hit publish.

Remember: the goal isn't perfection. The goal is movement based on informed commitment.

What's Coming Next

Learning to make confident, aligned decisions unlocks massive momentum. But choosing isn't the end of the story—it's the beginning. In the next chapter, we'll explore the habits and systems that turn decisions into consistent execution. You'll learn how to follow through, even when motivation fades—and build the kind of structure that supports real progress over time.

But for now: Choose. Commit. Move.

Success doesn't come from knowing more—it comes from doing more with what you already know.

If you are looking for a simple and powerful mental model to help you turn this chapter into real progress, try the "Why Roasted Roots" below. All the success shift recipes are located at http://www.yoursuccessshift.com/recipes to help you turn insight into momentum.

Why Roasted Roots

Purpose: Dig into your deeper purpose

Ingredients:

- 7 layers of inner why
- 2 cups of emotional honesty
- A sprinkle of legacy
- Optional: fire-roasted clarity

Method:

- Peel back each layer of your why.
- Roast with attention until truth softens you.
- Serve with integrity and intention.

Serving Suggestion:

- Pairs well with journaling in silence.

CHAPTER 5

LAZERCUTION—BUILDING RELENTLESS FOLLOW-THROUGH

"The only impossible journey is the one you never begin."

—Tony Robbins

From Burnout to Breakthrough – My Own Struggle with Follow-Through

For years, I wore my work ethic like a badge of honour. I believed that success was directly tied to how many hours I worked, how many tasks I ticked off, and how much energy I poured into my business. So I worked—hard. From 7 a.m. to 6 p.m., five (sometimes six) days a week, I built my accounting firm from the ground up.

And it worked. At least, on the surface.

The business grew. Revenue climbed. Clients came through the door and stayed. From the outside, it looked like I was thriving. Inside, I was anything but. Behind the scenes, I was overwhelmed and exhausted.

I kept everything in my head. No structured plan, no system—just mental juggling and constant reaction. I allowed interruptions to control my day:

phone calls, emails, team questions. I was reactive, not strategic—always putting out fires, never building the future. My office floor was littered with paper stacks: workshop notes, conference handouts, seminar materials—piles of potential I never had time to implement.

I had brilliant ideas. Bold strategies. I could see a better way of doing business—more efficient, more profitable, more fulfilling. But I didn't have the capacity to follow through on any of them.

I was spinning. Drowning in motion. And eventually, I hit a wall. I didn't love my business anymore. In truth, I resented it. I was ready to sell it and walk away. That was my wake-up call. I wasn't short on vision. I was short on execution. What I lacked wasn't motivation or creativity—it was discipline. I lacked Lazercution—the relentless focus to finish what truly mattered. And then, something shifted.

The Moment That Changed Everything

I attended a one-day accounting industry seminar and brought three of my team members along. At the time, I thought of it as a break—an escape from the daily chaos. But by the end of that day, something clicked. I saw it with absolute clarity: If I didn't change how I worked, I would never create the business I actually wanted to lead. The missing ingredient wasn't more effort. It wasn't about working harder. It was about working smarter.

What I needed was structure. Accountability. Systems that supported execution, not just ideas. So I made a decision that would change everything: I hired a coach. Over the next six months, we dismantled the chaos and rebuilt from the ground up. I introduced a shared digital diary so the whole team could see my availability. I blocked out time—actual, protected time—for deep work, client appointments, and uninterrupted focus. We implemented "quiet hours" during the day, where no one was allowed to interrupt unless it was urgent. I created "open-door" time in the afternoons for staff questions, so I wasn't pulled off-course every ten minutes. I hired an admin to handle tasks that didn't generate revenue. And finally, I tackled those piles of paper—I implemented the strategies I had once only dreamed about.

For the first time in years, I had breathing space, improved profits and a business I loved getting up in the morning to again. But the most powerful transformation came from one radical move that I fully embraced and gave other accounting practice owners the courage to do, because it worked. Something I am so proud of in my business journey and is one of my top stories that I share.

We eliminated timesheets, YES … those pesky administration-heavy, made-up timesheets; we ditched the constant struggle to have everyone operate in a 6-minute billing model and we introduced "value-based pricing". That single shift not only reshaped how we served our clients—it set us apart in the industry. We won innovation awards. We became more profitable than ever. And our clients felt the difference too. All of that began with one choice: to commit to focused execution. To practise Lazercution—the art of choosing what matters and finishing it, no matter what, and a few courage pills (just mints) to move forward and have fun in business.

Why Most Business Owners Struggle with Follow-Through

Ideas aren't the problem… finishing is.

Entrepreneurs get excited, set goals, get inspired… and then they rely on willpower instead of systems, react to whatever's urgent instead of prioritising what matters, and let their goals die a slow death in the shadow of busywork.

Here's the hard truth: If you don't control your schedule, your schedule will control you. Without Lazercution—focused, non-negotiable follow-through—chaos wins. And chaos never creates success.

The Execution Myth: Stop Waiting for Motivation

Most business owners say they just need to feel more motivated. How many times have you heard yourself or others say the following? They wait for the "right time".

"I'll start when things settle down."

"I'll do it when I'm more energised."

"I just need to feel more ready."

But motivation is inconsistent. What creates results is discipline. Top performers don't wait until they feel like doing the work. They create systems that make action inevitable.

This is Lazercution in motion:

- Commit first.
- Show up second.
- Feel good third.

The Discipline Shift: Becoming a Robot to Your Diary

If you want true freedom, here's your new rule: Become a robot to your diary. That means blocking out time for your most important work and treating that time like a meeting with your most valuable client... Not rescheduling. Not negotiating.

When the time comes, you don't argue. You act. It may feel strange at first. But within days, you'll see the difference. Because success doesn't come from doing a hundred things perfectly. It comes from doing the right things—consistently.

Reflection Prompt

My turning point didn't come from a new strategy—it came from learning to finish.

- Where in your own life or business are you starting without finishing?
- Where are you working hard, but not getting real results because nothing gets completed?

Write down one area where focused follow-through would change everything—and one step you could take today to bring Lazercution to it.

Your Success Shift Challenge: The 7-Day Lazercution Commitment

Ready to break the cycle?

Challenge: The 7-Day Lazercution Commitment

- Choose ONE high-impact project you've been avoiding.
- Block time in your diary every day for 7 days—even just 30 minutes.
- Show up like a robot. No rescheduling. No excuses.
- Reflect each evening: Did I keep my commitment?
- Reward yourself at the end of the week if you followed through.

One week of focused execution can create more momentum than months of planning.

Let Me Know How It Feels

When you complete your 7-Day Lazercution sprint, check in: What shifted? How did it feel to follow through instead of think about it? What did you finally complete that had been sitting still for too long?

Because once you prove to yourself that you can start, focus and finish—everything else becomes easier.

What's Coming Next

Lazercution is your foundation. But even the most disciplined mind will crumble without supportive systems.

In the next chapter, we'll explore how to build powerful structures that reinforce your focus—so you can stay on track, reduce decision fatigue, and scale without burning out.

Momentum without structure is exhausting. But momentum with structure? That's unstoppable.

If you are looking for a simple and powerful mental model to help you turn this chapter into real progress, try the "Micro-Promise Muffins" below. All the success shift recipes are located at http://www.yoursuccessshift.com/recipes to help you turn insight into momentum.

Micro-Promise Muffins

Purpose: Builds confidence in small daily doses

Ingredients:

- 1 tiny commitment
- 7 days of follow-through
- A dash of self-compassion
- Confidence crumbles on top

Method:

- Mix your promise with consistency.
- Bake daily—do not skip a day.
- Taste the growth with each bite.

Serving Suggestion:

- Best kept in plain sight. One muffin = one promise fulfilled.

CHAPTER 6

DISCIPLINE—THE ART OF TAKING ACTION DAILY

"You do not rise to the level of your goals. You fall to the level of your systems."

—James Clear, *Atomic Habits*

Why Most People Fail: The Illusion of Motivation

Everyone starts with good intentions. You set a goal. You feel excited. You take that first step with a sense of purpose and clarity. But then life happens. You wake up tired. A crisis pops up. The excitement that once lit you up quietly fades.

Suddenly, that goal—the one you swore you'd follow through on—feels less urgent. You tell yourself, "I'll get back to it tomorrow." But tomorrow becomes next week. Next week turns into next month. And before long, the dream gets filed away in the "someday" folder. The biggest mistake people make is believing success is powered by motivation. But motivation is like a spark—brilliant for a moment, but unreliable when the conditions change.

The real fuel behind lasting results?

Discipline.

- The kind that doesn't care how you feel in the moment.
- The kind that shows up anyway.
- The kind that builds systems where action is no longer optional—it's automatic.

Without discipline, your progress lives on a rollercoaster. With it, you build predictable, powerful results—day by day.

Anna's Story: From Overwhelm to Ownership

Anna grew up immersed in the rhythm of business. Her family owned a local accounting firm, and from a young age, she helped out—filing paperwork, answering phones, managing simple bookkeeping. She learned the ropes early, absorbing not only the work but the pride that came with serving clients well.

So, when her parents retired, it felt natural for Anna to take the reins. Clients trusted her. The staff admired her. On paper, she was the perfect successor. But the reality was far harder than she expected. Anna wasn't leading. She was reacting. Every day, she tried to be everything to everyone. She answered every staff question personally, even when they could have figured it out themselves. She jumped in to handle every small fire with clients. She said yes to every request, even when her schedule was bursting at the seams. She was constantly busy—but not productive. Her days stretched into 12-hour marathons. Weekends disappeared into "catch-up" time.

The spark that had once inspired her now barely flickered. "I feel like I'm holding up a collapsing building with my bare hands," she admitted to me in a coaching session. "No matter how much I give, it never feels like enough."

Anna didn't need more hours in the day. She needed boundaries. She needed structure. She needed discipline.

We started small. Anna created a daily leadership checklist—just three non-negotiable tasks. She blocked out 90 minutes each morning for deep work—no interruptions, no emails. She introduced a weekly team meeting where staff brought their problems all at once, instead of constantly knocking on her door.

At first, it felt rigid. Unnatural. Even uncomfortable. She worried she was being "too unavailable". She feared people might feel abandoned. But within just six weeks, everything changed. Clients were happier—because projects were delivered with more clarity and fewer delays. Staff became more independent—solving problems instead of passing them up the chain. Anna reclaimed her evenings and weekends—without guilt or fear that everything would fall apart. She found her energy again. Her clarity. Her leadership voice. Her breakthrough didn't come from more motivation. It came from building a system that made action consistent. Discipline didn't just rebuild her business. It gave her her life back.

Reflection: Anna's Story

Anna's turning point wasn't driven by motivation—it was created by discipline. By stepping into structure and letting go of the need to be everything to everyone, she reclaimed her leadership and her life.

- Where in your business or life are you choosing chaos over structure?
- What's one daily action—small but significant—you could commit to that would shift everything?
- Write it down. Block it out. Start today.

Discipline isn't about being perfect. It's about showing up anyway.

Why Discipline Beats Motivation Every Time

It's easy to believe that the most successful people are simply more inspired. That they wake up bursting with energy and vision. But that's not how success works. Olympic athletes don't always feel like training at 5:00 a.m. Best-selling authors don't always feel inspired to write the next page. Entrepreneurs don't always feel brave when making the tough decisions.

The difference? They act anyway—because they've built systems that support their goals, regardless of how they feel.

Motivation is a fair-weather friend. Discipline is a loyal companion.

Real-World Examples of Daily Discipline

- J.K. Rowling wrote the first Harry Potter book while struggling financially and raising a child. She didn't wait for perfect moments. She wrote in cafés, during naptimes and in between part-time jobs.
- Serena Williams continues to train rigorously—even after winning it all. When asked how she stays motivated, she said, "I train even when I don't want to."
- Warren Buffett built his investment empire not by chasing trends, but by quietly evaluating opportunities, reading for hours each day, and staying committed to the process—especially when others panicked.

None of them waited for inspiration. They trusted action over emotion.

The System for Daily Discipline

Discipline is like a muscle. It grows through practice, repetition and structure.

Here's a simple 4-step framework to help you build discipline that lasts:

Step 1: Treat Your Calendar as Law

- If it's not in your calendar, it doesn't exist.
- Block time for your most important work.
- Schedule it at the same time each day.
- Protect it like a non-negotiable client meeting.

Step 2: Create a "No Matter What" Rule

Commit to a daily action—big or small. Whether you feel like it or not, you show up. No skipping. No delays.

Step 3: Remove the Option to Fail

- Prepare your environment for success.
- Silence your phone. (I know … and it works!)
- Clear your workspace.
- Eliminate temptations.

Make doing the work easier than avoiding it.

Step 4: Reward Discipline, Not Just Results

Don't just celebrate outcomes—celebrate consistency.

Showing up daily is a win in itself.

A Second Story: Steve's 7-Day Breakthrough

Steve ran a boutique marketing agency. His ideas were sharp, but his execution was inconsistent. Every day started with email chaos, and every afternoon ended with frustration. Big projects kept being pushed aside for "urgent" distractions. So he tried something radical.

The 7-Day "No Matter What" Plan: He blocked 8:00-9:00 a.m. for marketing strategy—phone off, email closed. He committed to taking one deliberate action every day, no matter what. By the end of the week, he had:

- Completed two long-delayed marketing campaigns
- Signed two new clients
- Regained a sense of control

"It wasn't about working harder," he said. "It was about working deliberately."

Your Success Shift Challenge: The 7-Day "No Matter What" Plan

Challenge: Build Your Discipline Muscle Over the Next 7 Days

- Choose one key action you've been avoiding.
- Schedule it at the same time each day.
- Commit to it daily—no matter what.
- Prepare your environment for success
- Set a meaningful reward for completing all 7 days.

Why seven days?

Because short, focused bursts of discipline build long-term momentum. Neuroscience shows that new habits form fastest when they're daily and simple.

Let Me Know How It Feels

When you finish your 7-day plan, ask yourself:

- How did your focus shift?
- What changed in your confidence?
- What opened up because you showed up—even when you didn't feel like it?

Because discipline isn't about grinding harder. It's about choosing what matters—and honouring that choice every single day.

What's Coming Next

Discipline helps you build powerful habits. But what happens when your commitment is tested? When others doubt you? When fear rises? That's when courage becomes your next edge.

In the next chapter, we'll explore how to act boldly—even when it's unpopular, uncertain or scary.

If you are looking for a simple and powerful mental model to help you turn this chapter into real progress, try the "Bold Choice Chili" below. All the success shift recipes are located at http://www.yoursuccessshift.com/recipes to help you turn insight into momentum.

Bold Choice Chili

Purpose: Turn hesitation into heat

Ingredients:

- 1 delayed decision
- A spoonful of fear (adds spice!)
- 24-hour commitment window
- Optional: dash of accountability

Method:

- Throw in your stuck choice.
- Stir in courage and simmer with heat.
- Decide, take one action, Serve while hot

Serving Suggestion:

Do not refrigerate. Boldness fades when left overnight.

CHAPTER 7

COURAGE — CONTINUING WHEN THERE IS NO AGREEMENT

"Courage is resistance to fear, mastery of fear—not absence of fear."

—Mark Twain

The Business Owner Who Took the Leap Anyway

When I sold my accounting practice, it seemed like the logical next step. To others, it looked seamless—going from running a successful firm to mentoring other business owners full-time. But the truth underneath wasn't seamless at all. It was scary. It was uncertain. And it took every ounce of courage I had.

Accounting was safe. It was familiar. It was something I could do with my eyes closed. My clients had been with me for 10-15 years—some from the very beginning. I didn't need to hunt for leads. Work came in consistently through word-of-mouth. It was the business equivalent of running a bank: reliable, predictable, secure. And I was good at it.

But deep down, I knew I had outgrown it. There was a whisper inside me—one that grew louder each year. It told me I was meant for something more. I wanted to help business owners not just survive—but truly thrive. I wanted to teach them how to escape overwhelm, how to create clarity, how to build businesses that gave them both profit and peace.

But that meant letting go of my comfort zone. It meant leaving the safety of spreadsheets and stepping into a world where nothing was guaranteed. It meant becoming a coach. A guide. A speaker. A leader. Roles I didn't feel naturally suited for but were in my DNA… and needed to be explored.

Public speaking made my stomach churn. Sales conversations made my palms sweat (although I provided solutions for my clients every day, I had never put that down as sales), and lead generation? Well, that felt like climbing a mountain without a map.

I had to learn a whole new skillset:

- How to speak in front of a room without hiding behind a podium. At this stage, I was a shy accountant who loved the comfort of my desk and spreadsheets.
- How to ask powerful questions instead of giving step-by-step answers and solutions.
- How to build trust without the safety net of past credibility.
- How to generate leads and convert them—not just hope referrals that came in.

It was more than a career pivot. It was a complete identity shift and, despite the nerves, despite the unknowns, despite the lack of agreement from those around me who didn't fully understand the transition—I stepped forward.

Because I knew this one truth: If I stayed where I was, I would shrink. If I stepped forward, I could serve. So I chose to leap. It wasn't perfect. It wasn't smooth. But it was right. And every day since, I've been grateful I had the courage to act—not because I was fearless, but because I was willing to move even while afraid.

That's what courage really is.

Why Courage Matters More Than Confidence

Most people wait for confidence before they act.

"I'll launch when I feel ready."

"I'll speak up when I'm sure I won't fail."

"I'll take the leap when I feel more experienced."

But confidence isn't the starting point—it's the outcome. You don't build confidence by thinking. You build it by doing. Courage comes first. Confidence follows.

Every bold move you admire—every leader, every innovator, every entrepreneur you look up to—began with someone taking action before they felt ready. Courage is the bridge between fear and results.

The 3 Levels of Courage in Business

Courage isn't a one-time leap. It's a muscle you build and rebuild—again and again—as your business evolves. Here are the three levels of courage every entrepreneur must face:

Level 1: The Courage to Start

This is where most people stop. Starting means leaving what's known for what's possible. It's sending the first proposal. Posting your first piece of content. Attending your first networking event, even when you feel like a complete imposter. This kind of courage is raw. Vulnerable. Shaky. But it's the doorway to everything you want.

Level 2: The Courage to Keep Going

Starting is hard. But continuing—when the results don't come right away—is often harder. This is the courage to:

- Keep refining your offer when no one bites.
- Keep showing up when you feel invisible.
- Keep believing in your value—even when others don't yet see it.

This is where most people give up. But those who press on? They find momentum waiting on the other side of consistency.

Level 3: The Courage to Scale and Lead

Success doesn't make courage unnecessary—it demands more of it. As your business grows, so do the challenges. Saying no to good opportunities so you can pursue great ones. Letting go of control and trusting your team. Taking a stand for your values—even when it's unpopular. Leadership is not about having all the answers. It's about having the courage to keep choosing what matters.

Famous Examples of Courageous Action

Every game-changing idea started with doubt, resistance, and disbelief.

- Airbnb: People laughed at the concept. "Who would let strangers sleep in their home?" Today, it's worth billions.
- Netflix: Critics dismissed it. "Why stream movies when Blockbuster is around the corner?" Netflix didn't just survive—it reinvented entertainment.

- Spanx (Sara Blakely): Started with $5,000 and a bold idea. Manufacturers turned her away. Executives mocked her. Now, she's a billionaire who changed an entire industry.

If everyone agrees with you, you're probably playing too small. True leaders move before the world catches up.

How to Build Courage as a Daily Habit

Courage isn't something you find—it's something you create, one small brave act at a time. Here's how to build your courage muscle daily:

1. Expect Resistance

If you think everyone will cheer you on, you'll be disappointed. Expect hesitation. Expect criticism. Expect discomfort. That's not failure. That's the path.

2. Separate Rejection from Reality

Other people's opinions are not facts. Their doubt is about them, not you. Rejection doesn't mean you're wrong. It means you're ahead of the curve.

3. Take One Scary Action Each Day

Reach out to the client you've been avoiding. Post that story you've been holding back. Follow up—even if they didn't respond the first time. You don't have to leap every day. But you do have to move. Because small courageous actions stack up—until one day, you realise you've become someone who moves in the face of fear.

Reflection Prompt: When There Is No Agreement

My decision to leave the safety of accounting wasn't met with unanimous approval. People didn't understand. Some questioned it. Others stayed silent. But I moved anyway—because I was clear on why I was doing it and trusted my own ability and past successes to know that "everything will work out". I didn't know how; I just knew and I also knew it wasn't going to kill me, so it was worth the chance…

Now, it's your turn to reflect:

- Where in your life or business are you waiting for agreement, approval or reassurance before you act?
- What would you do today if you stopped waiting and simply chose to move forward—with or without the applause?

Write it down. Then do it scared. Your courage is more powerful than their permission.

If you are looking for a simple and powerful mental model to help you turn this chapter into real progress, try the "Lazercution Omelette" below. All the success shift recipes are located at http://www.yoursuccessshift.com/recipes to help you turn insight into momentum.

Lazercution Omelette

Purpose: Nourish your follow-through muscle

Ingredients:

- 3 eggs of structure
- 1 chopped non-negotiable

- Daily time blocks (sliced fine)
- Salt of "no matter what"

Method:

- Crack structure into your calendar.
- Fold in routines.
- Cook with discipline, not motivation.

Serving Suggestion:

- Best consumed early in the day, before distractions take over.

CHAPTER 8

SAYING NO TO DISTRACTIONS, SAYING YES TO YOUR MISSION

"The difference between successful people and really successful people is that really successful people say no to almost everything."

—Warren Buffett

The Business Owner Who Was Always Busy, But Never Moved Forward

Sarah was the kind of business owner people admired. She was energetic, smart, and constantly in motion—juggling meetings, interviews, collaborations and client requests with what looked like effortless grace. But five years into running her boutique marketing agency, Sarah felt like she was treading water. Her calendar was full. Her to-do list never ended. Her inbox overflowed with opportunities. She said yes to everything—guest podcasts, strategic partnerships, blog contributions, free consultations, volunteer committees. She wanted to build her brand, serve others, and be seen as someone who always showed up.

But underneath the surface, something wasn't right. Her revenue was flat. Her team was stretched thin. And her core business—the meaningful, high-impact work she had launched her company to deliver—was stuck in place.

One afternoon, during a coaching session, a mentor asked her a question that pierced through the noise: "Are you building your dream—or helping everyone else build theirs?" That moment changed everything. Sarah realised that her calendar wasn't a reflection of her mission. It was a reflection of other people's agendas.

She was living in reaction mode—saying yes out of guilt, obligation, or fear of missing out. She was available to everyone… except for herself. So she made a powerful shift. Within a few short weeks, Sarah began cancelling low-value meetings. She ruthlessly prioritised the three areas that drove real results in her business. And, most importantly, she began saying no—confidently, consistently and unapologetically.

The results were astonishing. In just 12 months, Sarah's business revenue increased by 60%. Not because she did more—but because she did less of what didn't matter and more of what did. By fiercely protecting her energy and focus, Sarah finally stepped into the next level of leadership—and success—she had been chasing for years.

Why Saying "No" Is Your Greatest Superpower

Most people believe success comes from working harder. But real success comes from working harder on the right things—and having the courage to say no to the rest. Every "yes" has a hidden cost. Each time you say yes to a small distraction, you might be saying no to your biggest goal—without even realising it.

A no to distractions is a yes to your vision.

A no to low-value tasks is a yes to high-impact work.

A no to someone else's urgency is a yes to your long-term mission.

Take Warren Buffett, one of the most successful investors in history. He once said he owes much of his success to the investments he didn't make. He lives by what he calls the "20-Slot Rule"—the idea that you should treat your entire life as if you only get 20 investments. If you could only say yes 20 times, how carefully would you choose?

Jeff Bezos operates the same way. Bezos protects his mornings from all distractions. No meetings. No calls. No interruptions. That's when his most powerful, innovative thinking happens—and Amazon's biggest ideas have been born during those protected hours.

Saying no isn't rude. It's responsible leadership. It's how you protect your mission from being diluted by noise.

My Own Battle with Saying No

Earlier in my career, I fell into the same trap Sarah did. I said yes to everything: Every coffee meeting. Every networking invite. Every "quick favour". Every shiny new idea or opportunity.

I told myself I was building my network. I told myself it was good for visibility. But behind the scenes, I was overwhelmed, distracted and constantly running behind on the things that truly mattered. The work that could grow my business— the deep, strategic, high-leverage work—kept getting pushed to "later". And "later" rarely came.

The turning point came when I realised that every yes to a distraction was a quiet no to my dreams. I wasn't moving forward—I was just staying busy. So I made a powerful decision. I identified my top three priorities for the business.

I created a "No List"—a document where I clearly outlined the kinds of requests I would decline, guilt-free. And I blocked out time in my calendar for focused, distraction-free work—and treated that time as sacred. At first, saying no was uncomfortable. But something remarkable happened: My clarity returned. My confidence rose. My results multiplied. Saying no didn't just protect my time. It protected my future.

How to Ruthlessly Protect Your Time

Saying no isn't about being harsh. It's about being clear—about your mission, your values, and your priorities. Here's how to start strengthening your No muscle today:

1. Identify Your Top 3 Priorities

Not everything matters equally. What three activities, if done consistently, would create 80% of your business growth? Maybe it's deep client work, developing a scalable product, or building partnerships or systems.

Write them down. Keep them visible. Use them as a decision-making filter. If something doesn't align, it's a no—or at least a "not right now".

2. Create a No List

This is a running list of tasks, requests, and obligations that you will intentionally decline moving forward. Some examples:

- Unpaid speaking gigs with no strategic value
- Coffee chats without a clear purpose
- Last-minute volunteer requests that don't align with your focus

This list takes the pressure off. It gives you clarity and boundaries in advance—so you're not stuck making tough calls in the moment.

3. Block Deep Work Time

Every day, schedule 90-120 minutes of uninterrupted time for your most valuable work. During this time:

- Turn off notifications
- Put your phone in another room
- Let your team or family know you're unavailable

Protect this time like your future depends on it—because it does.

Steve Jobs was famous for eliminating distractions. When he returned to Apple, he didn't just cut meetings—he cut most of Apple's product line, narrowing it down to four. That focus saved the company. Your focus will save your business too.

Famous Examples of Saying No to Say Yes

- Warren Buffett: Says no to 99% of opportunities. It's how he keeps his focus razor-sharp.
- Steve Jobs: Simplified Apple's entire strategy to just a handful of products.
- Jeff Bezos: Blocks mornings for deep thinking— no meetings allowed.
- Oprah Winfrey: Credits her success to learning the power of saying no and protecting her time with fierce intention.

Their results came not from doing more—but from doing less with far more focus.

Reflection Prompt: Your Personal No Audit

- Where are you saying yes when you should be saying no?
- What types of requests drain your energy but deliver little return?
- What's the "busywork" that distracts you from your most important projects?
- What's one meeting, event, or task you could decline or delegate this week?

Write them down. Audit your commitments. Then ask yourself: "Is this building my dream—or someone else's?"

Your Success Shift Challenge: Build Your No Muscle

Challenge: The No Muscle Plan

- Cancel or decline three current commitments that don't serve your top priorities.
- Create your No List. Start today. Add to it weekly.
- Schedule one 90-minute-deep work block every day for the next 7 days.

Examples:

- Say no to a low-value networking event
- Exit a group chat that drains your attention
- Cancel a meeting with no agenda or clear purpose

Every no to distraction is a yes to your dream.

Your Focus Is Your Future

There will always be another email. Another invite. Another request. But you must choose: You can either build your dream—or constantly be recruited into building someone else's. The most successful people protect their time like treasure. Because it is.

When you master the art of saying no—with clarity, grace and conviction—you reclaim the power to focus on what really matters. That's when momentum arrives. That's when clarity floods in. That's when results explode.

What's Coming Next

Now that you've reclaimed your time and strengthened your focus, it's time to shift how you view failure. Because in the next chapter, you'll discover the truth: Failure is not the opposite of success—it's the path to it. We'll explore how to turn failures into fuel—and why the most successful entrepreneurs treat setbacks as stepping stones to breakthroughs.

Are you ready?

If you are looking for a simple and powerful mental model to help you turn this chapter into real progress, try the "Focus Salad" below. All the success shift recipes are located at http://www.yoursuccessshift.com/recipes to help you turn insight into momentum.

Focus Salad

Purpose: Say no to noise, yes to nourishment

Ingredients:

- 3 leaves of clarity
- 1 scoop of bold boundaries
- A few tossed distractions (discarded!)
- Dressing: your mission statement

Method:

- Remove expired obligations.
- Toss in what energises you.
- Drizzle with mission-aligned action.

Serving Suggestion:

- Eat mindfully. No phones, no pings, no apologies.

CHAPTER 9

FAILURE AS FUEL – THE SECRET TO LONG-TERM SUCCESS

"I have not failed. I've just found 10,000 ways that won't work".

—Thomas Edison

The Business Owner Who Was Afraid to Fail—Until They Realised This

Mark had always dreamed of launching his own website agency. He was smart, capable and diligent. With years of corporate experience under his belt, he had the technical know-how, the people skills and the hunger to make something of his own. But when it came to stepping out from the safety of employment and into the unknown of entrepreneurship—he froze.

He spent months tinkering with his website. He filled notebooks with ideas, attended workshops, and polished his branding. He printed shiny new business cards and practiced his elevator pitch. But there was one thing he didn't do—he didn't launch. He didn't ask for the sale. He didn't promote his services. He didn't press go.

Underneath the preparation was a powerful fear—fear of failure. "What if no one buys?"; "What if I look foolish?"; "What if I fail and everyone sees it?" Finally, one of his mentors sat him down and said something simple—

but profound: "Mark, failure isn't the opposite of success. It's the path to it. You have to be willing to fail forward—and faster."

That moment shifted something in him. He stopped waiting for perfection. He stopped protecting himself from disappointment. He decided to act—imperfectly, but decisively.

Mark launched his first offer. Some people said yes. Many said no. He ran webinars. Some were completely empty. Others led to paying clients. He adjusted his services based on feedback, not fantasy. He learned to listen to the market, rather than trying to control it.

Two years later, Mark was running a thriving website agency with a steady flow of high-quality clients. He attributes his success to one thing—not his strategy, not his branding, not his skills. His relationship with failure.

He learned to stop fearing it and start learning from it. He used failure as fuel.

Why Failure Is Your Greatest Teacher

Failure is not the enemy. In fact, the most successful people in history have one thing in common: they failed—a lot. But they failed intelligently.

Every failure has value:

- It tells you what doesn't work.
- It forces you to sharpen your offer and your message.
- It humbles you—and grows your resilience.
- It accelerates your learning in ways success never can.

The bigger your vision, the more failure you will face. Not because you're doing something wrong—but because you're doing something bold. Thomas Edison famously made over 10,000 unsuccessful attempts before inventing the lightbulb. When asked about his countless failures, he said: "I have not failed. I've just found 10,000 ways that won't work."

Failure was not a setback. It was the process. And that's the key: Failure isn't the opposite of winning. It's the bridge that gets you there.

The Cost of Playing It Safe

Most business owners believe their greatest risk is trying and failing. But that's not true. The real risk is never trying at all.

When you avoid failure at all costs:

- You stay stuck in research and "getting ready".
- You miss out on priceless real-world feedback.
- You move slowly—while others take imperfect action and pull ahead.

Playing it safe feels smart. It feels responsible. But it quietly kills momentum—and your dream. Success doesn't come from overthinking. It comes from iteration, velocity, and movement through failure.

How to Redefine Failure So It Serves You

If you want to create long-term success, you need to reframe what failure means. Here's how:

1. See Failure as Data

Failure doesn't mean something is wrong with you. It simply means you've received new information.

Ask yourself:

- What worked?
- What didn't?
- What can I try differently?

Treat your actions like experiments. Adjust and repeat.

2. Separate the Event from Your Identity

Just because a product failed doesn't mean that *you* are a failure. You are not your outcomes. You are your effort. You are your growth. High performers understand this. They do not collapse emotionally over a poor launch, an empty workshop or a rejected pitch. They gather feedback, pivot, and move forward.

3. Set "Failure Goals"

Don't just aim for wins. Aim for action.

Try goals like:

- "I'll make 20 offers this month—even if 18 are no's."
- "I'll pitch 10 podcasts—even if 9 say no."
- "I'll post a video every day this week—even if no one comments."

The more you expose yourself to potential failure, the more you expose yourself to real growth.

Famous Examples of Failing Forward

- Thomas Edison: 10,000 experiments before inventing the lightbulb.
- Walt Disney: Fired from a newspaper job for having "no imagination".
- J.K. Rowling: Rejected by 12 publishers before Harry Potter found a home.
- Henry Ford: Failed at multiple car companies before revolutionising transport.

Each of them failed. Each of them was told "no". But none of them stopped.

The Three Levels of Failure You Must Master

Level 1: Failure to Launch

This is the fear of starting. You tell yourself you're "not ready" yet.

Solution: Launch anyway. Start messy. Learn on the move.

Level 2: Failure in Growth

This happens when something doesn't go as planned: A campaign flops. A client cancels. A new idea doesn't land.

Solution: Adapt fast. Refine. Relaunch better.

Level 3: Failure in Leadership

This is the hardest level—when your decisions affect others.

You'll: Hire the wrong person. Say yes when you should've said no. Lose money on a strategy that once looked brilliant.

Solution: Zoom out. Keep perspective. Hold the vision bigger than the stumble.

Reflection Prompt: Your Failure Audit

Ask yourself:

- Where am I playing it safe because I'm afraid to fail?
- What opportunities am I avoiding because I might get rejected?
- What would I do this week if I were willing to fail—and learn?

Write down your answers. Let them be your map—not your prison.

Your Success Shift Challenge: Build Your Failure Tolerance

Challenge for This Week:

- Identify one area where fear of failure is holding you back
- Take one bold, imperfect action in that area
- Journal your lessons each evening—not your mistakes, your learnings

Examples:

- Pitch a service even if you're unsure they'll say yes
- Launch a beta version of a new offer
- Post a video—even if you're nervous to be seen

Your goal this week isn't perfection. It's progress.

Your Future Belongs to Those Who Fail Forward

Most people let failure stop them. But those who succeed? They use failure as rocket fuel. When you fail fast and fail forward: You grow faster than your peers. You build resilience that no course or coach can teach. You become unshakeable. You are not defined by your rejections, flops or missed shots. You are defined by your ability to get back up—wiser, stronger and more committed than ever.

Rise. Refine. Repeat. That's how long-term success is built.

What's Coming Next

Now that you've learned to turn failure into fuel, it's time to shift gears again. Because in the next chapter, we will explore the secret to unstoppable momentum—and why small, consistent action beats occasional brilliance every time. Are you ready to build habits that carry your vision all the way to reality? Let's go.

If you are looking for a simple and powerful mental model to help you turn this chapter into real progress, try the "Fail-Forward Pasta" below. All the success shift recipes are located at http://www.yoursuccessshift.com/recipes to help you turn insight into momentum.

Fail-Forward Pasta

Purpose: Turn missteps into momentum

Ingredients:

- 1 failed launch (cooked al dente)
- Sauce made from insights and review
- A sprinkle of resilience cheese
- Optional: fresh regret—rinse well first

Method:

- Boil the failure, extract the learning.
- Mix into new strategy.
- Plate with pride—it's progress.

Serving Suggestion:

- Serve warm. Share your story. Let others taste the truth.

CHAPTER 10

LIGHTING THE PATH FOR OTHERS

"Leadership is not about being in charge. It is about taking care of those in your charge".

—Simon Sinek, *Leaders Eat Last*

The Business Owner Who Transitioned from Doer to Leader

When Rachel launched her online design business, she wore every hat imaginable. She designed every client project, handled every invoice, replied to every customer email, and posted every piece of content on social media. She was proud of being "hands-on". Her clients loved how involved she was. In those early days, her business thrived on personal attention and hustle. But as her reputation grew, so did the workload.

What once felt like control began to feel like chaos. Rachel was drowning in tasks, working 80-hour weeks. She missed birthdays and weekends. Her laptop was her constant companion—even on holidays. She was exhausted. But what scared her more than burnout was the idea of letting go. Every time she thought about getting help, fear crept in: "What if they mess it up?"; "No one will do it as well as I do."; "It'll take more effort to train someone than just doing it myself."

One night, after pulling an all-nighter to deliver a project for a client who wasn't even her ideal target anymore, she hit her breaking point. Rachel looked around her office, cluttered with coffee cups and overdue tasks, and realised something painful: She wasn't building a business anymore. She was keeping herself trapped in a self-made prison. So she made a bold decision: She would lead—not just do.

Rachel hired an assistant. Then a junior designer. Then a client support manager. At first, letting go was difficult. She hovered over everything. Double-checked every piece of work. Corrected small errors without teaching. But over time, something shifted. Rachel stopped controlling. She started coaching. She created systems, gave feedback, and let people grow. And her team? They rose to the occasion.

Two years later, Rachel's business had tripled its revenue. She worked a manageable 30 hours a week, spent weekends with her family, and led a team that felt empowered and inspired. Because Rachel made the shift from "I'll do it all" to "I'll lead us forward." She learned to light the path—not carry the whole load.

Why Leadership Is the Final Step in Execution Mastery

Execution starts with you. But if it ends with you, your business will always be limited. Real leadership isn't about having authority—it's about: Creating conditions where execution thrives. Empowering others to act with ownership. Being the example, not just giving instructions.

You can't scale a mission if you're the only one moving it forward. At some point, real growth means helping others become capable, confident and committed executors in their own right.

What Leadership Is Not

There are three common myths that hold business owners back from true leadership.

1. Leadership Is Not Having All the Answers

Great leaders don't have every solution—but they ask the right questions. They draw out others' thinking and foster ownership, rather than dictating directions.

2. Leadership Is Not About Power

Power-driven leadership collapses over time. True leadership is built on influence—inspiring voluntary action through trust, vision and example.

3. Leadership Is Not Control

Micromanaging every detail stifles growth. When you set clear standards and then step back to coach instead of control, your team learns to solve problems, take initiative, and become leaders themselves.

How to Lead Through Execution

So, what does great leadership actually look like?

1. Be the First to Take Action

If you want your team to move fast, you move fast. If you want your clients to take risks, you take risks. Lead from the front—with clarity, courage and consistency.

2. Create a Movement, Not Just a Business

People don't rally behind products. They rally behind purpose. Rachel's team was loyal not just because of pay checks, but because of her mission—to help small business owners build brands they were proud of. What bigger purpose are you offering?

3. Mentor Others to Execute

Rachel stopped assigning tasks and started coaching execution. She taught her team how to think, how to prioritise, and how to take full ownership. The result? Her team started leading her business—not just working in it.

The Ripple Effect of Leadership

When you lead well, your impact multiplies. You don't just change your own outcomes—you elevate everyone around you. Your team grows under your mentorship. Your clients are inspired by your example. Your community is energised by your mission. Your family sees what real leadership looks like. You rise when you lift others.

Bringing Play into Leadership

Leadership doesn't have to be heavy. In fact, some of the most powerful cultures are grounded in play—curiosity, creativity and connection. Think of Pike Place Fish Market in Seattle. Known around the world for turning a repetitive, messy job into a joyful performance, Pike Place wasn't just about selling fish—it was about creating a culture of engagement. Customers laughed, threw fish, and returned with friends. Employees felt energised and valued. All because leadership encouraged play as part of the culture.

Play opens the door to creativity. Play builds trust. Play invites people to take bold action without the fear of being wrong. When you lead with lightness—not perfectionism—you make space for innovation, joy and momentum.

Famous Examples of Leadership Through Action

- Simon Sinek: Transformed the conversation on leadership from control to care.
- Howard Schultz: Prioritised employees at Starbucks, changing the industry standard.
- Fred Smith (FedEx): Built a culture where frontline workers were empowered to act.
- Brené Brown: Leads with vulnerability and trust, modelling courageous leadership worldwide.

These leaders don't just say what's right. They show it—consistently.

Action Challenge: Inspire One Person This Week

Your Challenge:

- Identify someone you can mentor, support or uplift.
- Take one small action—a message, a conversation, an opportunity.
- Celebrate their growth—not your role.

Examples:

- Acknowledge a team member's recent success
- Guide a junior colleague through a decision
- Reach out to an entrepreneur in your network who might need encouragement

Leadership isn't about being the hero. It's about building other heroes.

Leadership Is the Ultimate Execution Skill

Everything in this book has prepared you for this moment: Moving from knowing to doing. From fear to boldness. From overthinking to executing. From solo performer to builder of people.

True execution mastery is not what you do alone—it's what you make possible for others. When you build a culture of empowered execution, problems shrink. opportunities multiply, and results skyrocket.

You don't just lead a business. You lead a movement.

Final Reflection: Light the Path

Ask yourself:

- Who could grow under my mentorship?
- Where am I still holding on instead of empowering others?
- How can I lead with more play, trust, and purpose?

Leadership isn't about being the best. It's about bringing out the best in others.

If you are looking for a simple and powerful mental model to help you turn this chapter into real progress, try the "Legacy Layer Cake" below. All the success shift recipes are located at http://www.yoursuccessshift.com/recipes to help you turn insight into momentum.

Legacy Layer Cake

Purpose: Build impact that outlasts you

Ingredients:

- 1 base layer of aligned action
- Filling: values, voice, and visibility
- Topped with the ripple effect
- Optional sparkler: the people you inspire

Method:

- Build layer by layer, with intention.
- Pause between layers to reflect.
- Top with purpose and light it up.

Serving Suggestion:

- Best shared with those you mentor, lead or love.

FINAL CALL TO ACTION: THE SUCCESS SHIFT CHALLENGE

Now that you've reached the final chapter, it's time to make a decision.

Not later.

Not someday.

Now.

What to do:

- Choose one project, offer, or idea you've been holding back.
- Take visible action in the next 24 hours.
- Make a public commitment—post it, share it, declare it.
- Keep going—especially when it gets hard.

The world doesn't shift with good intentions. It shifts with leaders like you—taking bold, imperfect action and lighting the path for others.

Your Success Shift has already begun.

Now go lead it.

CONNECT WITH GLENIS

Glenis Gassmann is available for speaking engagements, workshops, interviews, and business mentorship programs.

🌐 Website: www.glenisgassmann.com

✉ Email: glenis@glenisgassmann.com

🖩 Phone: +61 0402 594 095

🔗 Follow on LinkedIn, Facebook, and Instagram

FOUND THIS BOOK VALUABLE?

If *Why Knowing Isn't Enough* gave you clarity, insight, or practical tools, the best way to support Glenis is to share it with someone who would benefit too.

You can also leave a short review on Amazon—your feedback helps others discover the book and take the leap from knowing… to doing.

Thank you for being part of this shift.

Warmly,

Glenis Gassmann

NOTES

NOTES

NOTES

NOTES

NOTES

NOTES

NOTES

NOTES

NOTES

NOTES